Birdy

By Monika Mundell

Birdy
by Monika Mundell

Copyright © 2011 by Monika Mundell

Editor: Davina Haisell
Cover & interior design: Blue Sun Studio, Inc.

ISBN: 1460941543

Preface

This is the true story of how Birdy, our beloved pet cockatiel, beat the odds and survived six weeks in the wild. I've wanted to write this book ever since she found her way back home. It's an ode to her and all the birds that live on this planet.

Birdy truly is a princess—an angel of sorts — disguised in a feathery body. She's not only pretty, she is smart, fun and the best companion a person could ever wish for. Birdy is a survivor!

My hope is to take you on a magical journey that is filled with inspiration and triumph, despite being sprinkled with a hearty dose of despair. The core message in this book is to never give up hope in times of personal grief and hardship.

If I can inspire just one person to believe in magic, and that the impossible can happen, I shall be very happy.

I want to dedicate this book to my beloved husband John, without whom I would have never had the strength to stay sane during those many dark weeks.

John, you are my rock. You are my soulmate. Thank you for your continuous support and for the love you give so selflessly.

I also want to thank my wonderful online friends for inspiring me to excel (you know who you are). You encourage me to be the best I can be.

Furthermore, I want to thank my wonderful copy editor and friend, Davina Haisell. You rock. Thanks for turning my words into a thrilling story. I'm humbled by your gentle, yet firm guidance.

To my readers, thank you for picking up a copy of this book and helping me spread the word about my wonderful friend, Birdy.

Monika Mundell,
Author

Foreword

We all experience adversity in our lives; some events are considered tragic and inconsolable, while others pass us by with little impact on our feelings. This real-life story shows the impact a pet can have on people who really care about their furry, feathered or scaly friends.

Monika and her husband, John, are obviously very dedicated to their pet "Birdy", a cockatiel. Many of us, including myself, have or are privileged to be able to care for this wonderful species.

This is a delightfully told story. For myself and other readers it is uplifting to know that there are many of us who genuinely care about our chargers, contrary to what we often read or hear in the media about neglect.

You will feel so much closer to the author and her family upon reading this great short story of heartache and perseverance. I am honoured to get to know Monika and her family through their experiences.

Peter Odekerken,
Author of *A Guide to Lories and Lorikeets*, published by Australian Birdkeeper.

Chapter One

It was a crisp spring day. The sun had just kissed the top of her rising journey and was lazily tipping toward the west. The world was at peace.

In the garden, magpies were warbling their distinctive song, butcher birds were whistling their ABCs, and the magpie-larks were screeching while busily searching for their flock. Monika was lying in a hammock on the back veranda, relaxing in the peaceful surroundings, feeling quite content.

Her husband, John, was inside getting ready for work, with Birdy riding proudly on his shoulder. They were enjoying spending quality time with each other. Birdy would often hitch a ride on either John's or Monika's shoulder, just because she could. She loved being carried around their home and sometimes even rode on their heads for extra fun.

It was a picture-perfect afternoon and a moment

when the world seemed to be at peace; a moment one would like to bottle up and save for eternity.

Suddenly, a high-pitched screech pierced the quiet afternoon. It was followed by a human scream of desperation as John rushed outside to the porch in a panic.

"Birdy! Come back...!"

There above the trees flew their Birdy, higher and higher in widening circles. Within seconds, she was nothing but a tiny speck of yellow, hard to distinguish from the colourful orange and yellow afternoon sky. John's eyes searched frantically, but he'd lost sight of her.

He sat down, seemingly frozen to their front porch, and clearly in shock. John couldn't believe what had just happened. His mind was overcome with thoughts of self-blame that swirled like a vicious tornado. He was stunned. Besides himself. Crying.

"What happened?" Monika shouted. She was sitting upright in her hammock, suddenly fearful.

"Birdy flew away!" was John's frantic response.

Shaking her head in disbelief, Monika ran to the front door and caught one last glimpse of Birdy as she swooped above the house. She flew higher and higher into the sky and then she was gone, leaving them with nothing... nothing except for John's cries of anguish.

"What the hell had just happened?" Thoughts screamed through their minds, but were silenced by disbelief and shock.

Only minutes ago, Birdy had languished on John's shoulder, watching him brush his teeth in their tiny family bathroom. Now, she was gone.

Monika couldn't quite fathom how John had opened the front door with Birdy on his shoulder, while he was brushing his teeth.

"How could he!?"

With Birdy having just disappeared and Monika now standing behind him, John came to his senses and sprang into action. He spun on his heels, raced from the porch, and with a few long strides up the road he disappeared from Monika's view. All she could hear were his frantic calls: "Birdy. Birdy. Birdy!"

Forced to face the grim reality that Birdy had flown away, Monika raced for her car keys and followed John in their old BJ40 Toyota Land Cruiser. A frantic search for Birdy began in their neighbourhood, and lasted well into late afternoon. Up and down their street, left and right through neighbouring streets, the search continued.

Only when long shadows of darkness slowly crept across their path, did the pair return home. Exhausted and burnt out, they were forced to call it a day.

Having returned to a much too quiet home, a home that was without its most precious inhabitant, the reality of the situation hit them hard. They cried... and cried... and cried.

Monika and John had developed a passionate love and respect for Birdy many years ago. When she entered their home as an unexpected addition to the family, she quickly became the centre of attention. The little yellow lutino cockatiel stole their hearts in just a few short weeks. They both loved her – to bits!

Now, with Birdy missing, their world had stopped turning. Gone were the colours of happiness and the sounds of love. Gone was their little yellow lutino.

Birdy's cage sat prominently in the living room, empty. There were remnants of food and water in her feeding containers. The house was still and strangely quiet, except for Monika's and John's cries of sorrow. They were devastated.

They would miss sharing evenings with Birdy, their little princess—watching TV, cuddling on the couch or playing catch-me-if-you-can on the computer keyboard. Their world had turned a gloomy shade of grey.

Monika wanted answers from John. "What in the world were you thinking to open the door with Birdy on your shoulder?" she asked accusingly.

"I was hot and needed some fresh air. I forgot that Birdy was sitting on my shoulder."

It was clear that John was heartbroken because of his mistake, and Monika was careful not to say something she might regret. But, the sudden loss of their coveted "princess Birdy" had hit her hard. She desperately wished she'd known about the unfolding drama before it had been too late.

"Oh, if only…"

John's explanation was filled with despair: "A large bird scared her with its cry. She took off in a fright and couldn't fly down. She really tried, but just couldn't land."

They both found it hard to believe that John had opened the front door, forgetting that Birdy was sitting on his shoulder. In the hellish weeks that followed and for many months later, John would repeatedly wake from a nightmare, drenched in sweat, his heart skipping beats in terror.

Chapter Two

Monika and John cried a lot that night and sleep was for the most part, elusive. When it eventually swept over them in broken shards of time, they found short-lived respite in a dream-spiked slumber. Waking in terror every hour or so, their ears were primed to listen for Birdy's voice, wondering if perhaps they could hear her call in the night.

The next morning the couple rose with jumbled thoughts—disbelief, sadness, anger and more tears. Frantically, they printed flyers from their home printer and began posting them with the ink barely dry. They spent the majority of that day and the rest of the week distributing those flyers on foot. No letterbox or shop in their coastal Queensland Township was spared.

Birdy had become somewhat of a local celebrity. Neighbours and strangers found themselves confronted with a cry for help when they checked their letterboxes. Monika and John never stopped calling out for Birdy while walking the streets.

Their days were worrisome; minutes passed, heavy with sadness, anger and disbelief. They closed each day, surrendering to tears and restless nights that were spent longing for their little feathery mate. Sleep was evasive until fatigue dropped them into a temporary slumber where yet another nightmare would take hold.

Over the weeks that ensued, countless telephone calls were received from locals wanting to help find Birdy. Many claimed to have spotted the little cockatiel nearby. Every lead was instantly and carefully followed up with a frenzied search around the reported location.

There was never any sign of Birdy, despite everyone's effort. Days passed; then weeks. Life went on. Life sucked.

In her heart, Monika felt that Birdy was still alive. The connection they shared was strong and she was convinced she would feel it if something terrible had happened. Trusting her gut feeling gave her hope.

John became withdrawn. He was angry and blamed himself for their loss. Monika understood that it wasn't his fault, but even though it had been an accident, she found it hard to be compassionate. She missed her princess so much, and wondered if life would ever be the same again.

Every day for the next two weeks, they combed the neighbourhood in search of their little yellow cockatiel, calling her name hundreds of times while walking the streets. They delivered flyers throughout the township, as far away as the outskirts of town, knowing that birds could fly long distances, especially when lost and frightened.

Strangers offered sympathetic words. They meant well, but their words were a small consolation for the couple. Some folk speculated that birds could survive in the wild for a long time. Friends shared wonderful survival stories about their lost pets, in the hopes of keeping Monika's and John's faith alive.

Realistically, Birdy's chances of survival were slim, as a myriad of natural predators lived in her hometown. Those predators flew, slithered across the ground and climbed trees; trees that Birdy might use for shelter at night.

She shared her new world with hawks, crows, butcher birds, magpies, snakes, possums and rats. The list was endless. Their hometown was a paradise for tourists, but a tiny, lost cockatiel would have to fight for survival, every minute and every hour of every day.

Birdy was native to Australia, but had been raised as a pet. She was used to being fed, and to survive in the wild she would have to fight for food and water, for shelter from the elements – and from her enemies.

Many more weeks passed without any sign of their beloved Birdy. Spring was coming to an end. Early signs of summer were glaringly apparent. The sun had become lazy in the sky, slowly making her journey from east to west every single day. The ocean was heating up. Late spring thunderstorms brought some respite to the thirsty land; perhaps even to Birdy, hoped Monika and John.

She was first and foremost on their minds as they woke each morning to embark on yet another day filled with sadness. Likewise, their last thought of the day was of Birdy, followed by a short call for help from the Universe.

Their life was permeated with thoughts about this wonderful creature who had become such an important part of their family. Who would have thought that Birdy, the little yellow cockatiel, could bring so much happiness and then so much grief into their lives?

Six weeks passed. They'd lost faith that Birdy would return home safely, and found themselves hoping she had been rescued by caring people. What was important to them was that she was alive, safe and happy.

Monika and John decided to buy another cocka-tiel to distract them from their overpowering grief. They wanted another bird to keep them company and hoped it would help to ease their sadness.

They visited several pet stores in search of a baby cockatiel, after agreeing they didn't want to buy a mature bird. Their new cockatiel would be young; one they would raise with lots of love and personal attention.

They were lucky in their search at the third store. Upon entering, Monika locked her eyes on Pumpkin, a baby cockatiel with distinctive plumage. She was sitting on her perch, screeching and vying for everyone's attention.

"Aww, look. John, how cute is this little munchkin!" Monika exclaimed, after watching her antics. "Do you think we can take her home?"

"Sure!" John replied. "She's too cute. Let's bring her home."

And so they did. After a quick transaction and some additional buys—baby formula, birdseed and toys for their new feathery friend —Pumpkin happily rode home with them in their Toyota.

The young cockatiel settled in her new home with ease and was soon spoiled with plenty of cuddles, baby formula and playtime. Monika and John were over the moon with their new little friend, knowing they had made the right choice in bringing Pumpkin home.

Still, despite their newfound happiness, they yearned for Birdy every single day, wondering where she could be.

Chapter Three

Monika was convinced that Birdy was still alive. She told John: "I know that Birdy is alive! I can feel it in my heart."

"Oh, do I wish for that to be true!" was John's earnest response.

They continued to receive reports from people claiming to have seen Birdy, all of which were dutifully followed up. Their hopes were dashed with each false alarm. Still, nothing. Still, no Birdy.

One Saturday, Monika spent a quiet evening alone at home while John was at work. A massive thunderstorm wreaked havoc that night. Lightning struck nearby several times in a row. Tree branches waved in powerful wind gusts. The ocean raged. It was a living hell.

Monika's thoughts were especially focused on Birdy: "Where was she? Did she have shelter?"

She knew that Birdy had plenty of water, thanks

to the rain. Before going to bed, Monika sent another call for help to the Universe.

The next morning all signs of the storm were diminished by bright sunshine. It was a picture-perfect day and since Sunday was John's day off, they wanted to make the most of it. Spending quality time with good people was a favourite past-time and high on their list of priorities, so they accepted an invitation to lunch at a friend's home.

Monika and John enjoyed a relaxing few hours with their friends, eating, chatting, and even laughing, occasionally. It was nice to feel alive again and they both shared this sentiment several times during the day, feeling pleasantly surprised.

Upon arriving home at around 6 p.m. that evening, they noticed the light on the answering machine was flashing.

There was a message!

They looked at each other in silence as hope bubbled up in their hearts. "Could it be...?"

Waiting for the message to rewind seemed like an eternity, and then... "Hi, my name's Peter," the recording said. "I think I might have found your Birdy...."

Monika picked up the phone instantly and dialled the number with shaky fingers.

When the phone was answered, she heard a man's voice: "Peter here."

"This is Monika," she almost whispered. "You called to say you might have found our Birdy?"

"Yes, I believe it's her," the voice said. "We picked up your flyer at the supermarket. The picture is identical."

"When can we come and see her?" Monika asked, barely stifling her excitement, afraid to get her hopes up.

"Now?!" Peter replied.

She hung up the phone after exclaiming a loud whoop of joy and turned to face John, smiling. They hugged. They danced. They cried. Renewed hope permeated their being with a force so strong it made them dizzy.

They jumped back in their Toyota and drove the short distance to Peter's home. After being greeted at the front door by his family, the couple entered the hallway, nervously.

And there she was!

As unbelievable as it seemed, the little yellow cockatiel trapped beneath Peter's laundry basket was indeed, Birdy. Monika recognized her instantly and likewise, Birdy recognized Monika.

"It's Birdy!" Monika exclaimed with delight. "It's my princess!"

She hugged Peter, and then John. They cried tears of joy. Once again Birdy and Monika were together—they were one.

After six weeks of living in the wild, against all

odds, Birdy had survived her ordeal. Peter's kids had found her in their backyard during the raging storm the night before, dripping wet and very weak. She had lost quite a bit of weight during her six-week adventure; nothing that couldn't be fixed with lots of love, a good diet and plenty of cuddles and rest.

True to the promise offered on their flyer, John gave Peter a generous reward. To Monika and John, Birdy was worth more than money could ever buy. They were quite happy to show their immense gratitude to Peter and his family.

Happily, and in loving arms, Birdy returned home that night in the old BJ40 Toyota Land Cruiser that had searched frantically for her on that first day.

Upon arriving home, Birdy exclaimed her joy with a trademark "peep." She knew she was home and safe at last. That night, Birdy enjoyed the most special homecoming a bird could ever wish for. There was tons of laughter, love and cuddles, and not to mention, lots of her favourite treats.

Despite being exhausted from her long adventure, she enjoyed the attention. The two happy "parents" cried tears of gratitude while they watched Birdy demonstrate her excitement with distinctive sounds and body movements.

The party was long-lasting. Birdy went to sleep late that night, as did Monika and John, exhausted but very happy and content. Their prayers had been answered. Life as they knew it was once again complete.

It was a happy ending for everyone. Monika, John... and Birdy, had their own wonderful survival story to tell.

Afterward

Four years later, Birdy is still the centre of Monika's and John's universe. Meanwhile, she has found true love with Romeo, a wonderful and gentle cockatiel. Together, they have parented two sets of babies: First, Spikey and Mini, then Billy Jean and Bubbles; two pairs of female/male siblings.

Bubbles, the younger male, is happily mated with Mickey, who came into their family from a breeder friend. Mini, the older male, has found love with Pumpkin, who joined their household during those horrible weeks when Birdy was missing. Spikey, the older female (Birdy's first-born), and Billy Jean, the younger female, are still living in the same "house" as their parents; they are a very close-knit bunch.

Their little home in the coastal Queensland Township is full of song, chatter, laughter, fun, playtime and cuddling. Birdy enjoys the special attention she receives every single day, from Monika and John, and from her mate, Romeo. And so she should. She deserves it!

86316285R00017

Made in the USA
Middletown, DE
29 August 2018